THE OXFORD
ILLUSTRATED
Book of
AMERICAN
CHILDREN'S
POEMS

THE OXFORD ILLUSTRATED

Book of

AMERICAN CHILDREN'S POEMS

Edited by

DONALD HALL

OXFORD
UNIVERSITY PRESS

OXFORD
UNIVERSITY PRESS

Oxford New York
Athens Auckland Bangkok Bogotá Bombay
Buenos Aires Calcutta Cape Town Dar es Salaam Delhi
Florence Hong Kong Istanbul Karachi
Kuala Lumpur Madras Madrid Melbourne
Mexico City Nairobi Paris Singapore
Taipei Tokyo Toronto Warsaw
and associated companies in
Berlin Ibadan

Copyright © 1999 by Donald Hall
Published by Oxford University Press, Inc.
198 Madison Avenue, New York, New York 10016

Library of Congress Cataloging-in Publication Data
The Oxford illustrated book of American children's poems/edited by Donald Hall.
p. cm. Includes index.
Summary: An anthology of American poems, arranged chronologically,
from colonial alphabet rhymes to Native American cradle songs to contemporary poems.
ISBN 0-19-512373-5 (alk. paper)
1. Children's poetry, American. [1. American poetry collections.] I. Hall, Donald, 1928– .
PS586.3.O95 1998
811.008'09282--dc21   99-34419
CIP

9 8 7 6 5 4 3 2 1

Printed in Hong Kong

Design and layout: Nora Wertz
Picture research: Lisa Kirchner

On the cover: Illustration by Jessie Willcox Smith, 1905,
from *A Child's Garden of Verses* by Robert Louis Stevenson.
Frontispiece: Unpublished illustration by John R. Neill, 1914,
for Robert Louis Stevenson's *Treasure Island.*

CONTENTS

PREFACE

by Donald Hall

Poetry for our children began with Native American cradle songs, moved on to a rhymed alphabet, bloomed in the 19th century with "A Visit from St. Nicholas," expanded in the 20th, and continues with vigor into the 21st. Many children's magazines of the 19th and early 20th centuries required verses for recitation, for laughter, or for sleepiness at bedtime. Some of the best of these poems have gradually disappeared.

Here we mean to bring them back into light. In the larger, unillustrated *Oxford Book of Children's Verse in America,* the present editor assembled a history of the genre and chose poems that parents could read aloud to their children. This second selection, with archival illustrations, returns many poems to the scenes of their origin. The editor hopes that adults will read these poems aloud to small children and show them the pictures. He also hopes that when these children start reading, they will continue to take pleasure in this book, speaking aloud the sounds of poetry—and learning poems by heart. Poetry is most poetry when it makes noise. With an old picture beside it, a poem may also preserve a moment of the American past.

ANONYMOUS NATIVE AMERICAN

Chant to the Fire-Fly

Fire-fly, fire-fly, light me to bed.
Come, come, little insect of light,
You are my candle, and light me to go.

She Will Gather Roses

This little girl
only born to
gather wild roses.
Only born to
shake the wild rice loose
with her little fingers.
Only to collect the sap
of young hemlocks
in spring. This woman–
child was only born
to pick strawberries,
fill baskets with
blueberries, soapberries,
elderberries. This
little girl was
only born to
gather wild roses.

Mother's Song to a Baby

First
this little baby
has been given life
through the medicine man's song
through the medicine man's
    prayer
for this baby the songs
have been sung

Next
the baby's mother
has taken care of him
with the songs of the rain gods

This
little baby
in his cloud-cradle
was watched over
by his mother

It
was
nice
how the clouds
came up like foam
and
as if he
was among them
this little baby
was cared for

Alphabet

In Adam's fall
We sinned all.

Thy life to mend
This Book attend.

The Cat doth play
And after slay.

A Dog will bite
A thief at night.

An Eagle's flight
Is out of sight.

The idle Fool
Is whipped at school.

As runs the Glass
Man's life doth
    pass.

My book and
    Heart
Shall never part.

Job feels the rod
Yet blesses God.

Our King the good
No man of blood.

The Lion bold
The Lamb doth
    hold.

The Moon gives
    light
In time of night.

Nightingales sing
In time of spring.

The royal Oak was
    the tree
That saved his
    Royal Majesty.

Peter denies
His Lord and cries.

Queen Esther
comes in Royal
    State
To save the Jews
    from dismal fate.

Rachel does mourn
For her firstborn.

Samuel anoints
Whom God
    appoints.

Time cuts down all
Both great and
    small.

Uriah's beauteous
    wife
Made David seek
    his life.

Whales in the sea
God's voice obey.

Xerxes the great
    did die
And so must you
    and I.

Youth forward
    slips.
Death soonest nips.

Zaccheus he
Did climb the tree
His Lord to see.

CLEMENT CLARKE MOORE
1779–1863

A Visit from St. Nicholas

'Twas the night before Christmas, when all through the house
Not a creature was stirring, not even a mouse;
The stockings were hung by the chimney with care,
In hopes that St. Nicholas soon would be there;
The children were nestled all snug in their beds,
While visions of sugar-plums danced in their heads;
And mamma in her 'kerchief, and I in my cap,
Had just settled our brains for a long winter's nap—
When out on the lawn there arose such a clatter,
I sprang from my bed to see what was the matter.
Away to the window I flew like a flash,
Tore open the shutters, and threw up the sash.
The moon, on the breast of the new-fallen snow,
Gave the lustre of midday to objects below;
When, what to my wondering eyes should appear,
But a miniature sleigh and eight tiny reindeer,
With a little old driver, so lively and quick,
I knew in a moment it must be St. Nick.
More rapid than eagles his coursers they came,
And he whistled, and shouted, and called them by name:
"Now, *Dasher!* now, *Dancer!* now, *Prancer* and *Vixen!*
On, *Comet!* on, *Cupid!* on, *Donder* and *Blitzen!*
To the top of the porch! to the top of the wall!
Now dash away! dash away! dash away all!"
As dry leaves that before the wild hurricane fly,
When they meet with an obstacle, mount to the sky;
So up to the house-top the coursers they flew
With the sleigh full of toys, and St. Nicholas too.
And then, in a twinkling, I heard on the roof
The prancing and pawing of each little hoof—

As I drew in my head, and was turning around,
Down the chimney St. Nicholas came with a bound.
He was dressed all in fur, from his head to his foot,
And his clothes were all tarnished with ashes and soot;
A bundle of toys he had flung on his back,
And he looked like a pedlar just opening his pack.
His eyes—how they twinkled; his dimples, how merry!
His cheeks were like roses, his nose like a cherry!
His droll little mouth was drawn up like a bow,
And the beard of his chin was as white as the snow;
The stump of a pipe he held tight in his teeth,
And the smoke it encircled his head like a wreath;
He had a broad face and a little round belly
That shook, when he laughed, like a bowl full of jelly.
He was chubby and plump, a right jolly old elf,
And I laughed when I saw him, in spite of myself;
A wink of his eye and a twist of his head
Soon gave me to know I had nothing to dread;
He spoke not a word, but went straight
    to his work,
And filled all the stockings; then
    turned with a jerk,
And laying his finger aside of his
    nose,
And giving a nod, up the
    chimney he rose;
He sprang to his sleigh, to his
    team gave a whistle,
And away they all flew like the
    down of a thistle.
But I heard him exclaim, ere
    he drove out of sight,
*"Happy Christmas to all, and to
    all a good night!"*

ELIZA LEE FOLLEN
1787–1860

The Three Little Kittens

Three little kittens lost their mittens;
  And they began to cry,
    "Oh, mother dear,
    We very much fear
That we have lost our mittens."
    "Lost your mittens!
    You naughty kittens!
Then you shall have no pie!"
      "Mee-ow, mee-ow, mee-ow."
"No, you shall have no pie."
      "Mee-ow, mee-ow, mee-ow."

The three little kittens found their
  mittens;
  And they began to cry,
    "Oh, mother dear,
    See here, see here!
See, we have found our mittens!"
    "Put on your mittens,
    You silly kittens,
And you may have some pie."
      "Purr-r, purr-r, purr-r,
Oh, let us have the pie!
      Purr-r, purr-r, purr-r."

The three little kittens put on their
  mittens,
  And soon ate up the pie;
    "Oh, mother dear,
    We greatly fear

That we have soiled our mittens!"
    "Soiled your mittens!
    You naughty kittens!"
Then they began to sigh,
      "Mee-ow, mee-ow, mee-ow."
Then they began to sigh,
      "Mee-ow, mee-ow, mee-ow."

The three little kittens washed their
  mittens,
  And hung them out to dry;
    "Oh, mother dear,
    Do not you hear
That we have washed our mittens?"
    "Washed your mittens?
    Oh, you're good kittens!
But I smell a rat close by,
      Hush, hush! Mee-ow,
    mee-ow."
"We smell a rat close by,
      Mee-ow, mee-ow, mee-ow."

THE END

SARAH JOSEPHA HALE
1788–1879

Mary's Lamb

Mary had a little lamb,
  Its fleece was white as snow,
And everywhere that Mary went
  The lamb was sure to go;
He followed her to school one day—
  That was against the rule,
It made the children laugh and play
  To see a lamb at school.

And so the teacher turned him out,
  But still he lingered near,
And waited patiently about,
  Till Mary did appear.
And then he ran to her and laid
  His head upon her arm,
As if he said, "I'm not afraid—
  You'll shield me from all harm."

"What makes the lamb love Mary so?"
  The little children cry;
"Oh, Mary loves the lamb, you know,"
  The teacher did reply,
"And you each gentle animal
  In confidence may bind
And make it follow at your call,
  If you are always kind."

ANNA MARIA WELLS
1795–1868

The Cow-Boy's Song

"Mooly cow, mooly cow, home from the wood
They sent me to fetch you as fast as I could.
The sun has gone down: it is time to go home.
Mooly cow, mooly cow, why don't you come?
Your udders are full, and the milkmaid is there,
And the children all waiting their supper to share.
I have let the long bars down,—why don't you pass through?"
    The mooly cow only said, "Moo-o-o!"

"Mooly cow, mooly cow, have you not been
Regaling all day where the pastures are green?
No doubt it was pleasant, dear mooly, to see
The clear running brook and the wide-spreading tree.
The clover to crop, and the streamlet to wade,
To drink the cool water and lie in the shade;
But now it is night: they are waiting for you."
    The mooly cow only said, "Moo-o-o!"

"Mooly cow, mooly cow, where do you go,
When all the green pastures are covered with snow?
You go to the barn, and we feed you with hay,
And the maid goes to milk you there, every day;
She pats you, she loves you, she strokes your sleek hide,
She speaks to you kindly, and sits by your side:
Then come along home, pretty mooly cow, do."
    The mooly cow only said, "Moo-o-o!"

"Mooly cow, mooly cow, whisking your tail,
The milkmaid is waiting, I say, with her pail;
She tucks up her petticoats, tidy and neat,
And places the three-leggéd stool for her seat:—
What can you be staring at, mooly? You know
That we ought to have gone home an hour ago.
How dark it is growing! O, what shall I do?"
    The mooly cow only said, "Moo-o-o!"

LYDIA MARIA CHILD
1802–1880

The New-England Boy's Song about Thanksgiving Day

Over the river and through the wood,
　To grandfather's house we go;
　　　The horse knows the way
　　　To carry the sleigh
Through the white and drifted snow.

Over the river and through the wood—
　Oh, how the wind does blow!
　　　It stings the toes
　　　And bites the nose
As over the ground we go.

Over the river and through the wood,
　To have a first-rate play.
　　　Hear the bells ring,
　　　"Ting-a-ling-ding!"
Hurrah for Thanksgiving Day!

Over the river and through the wood
　Trot fast, my dapple-gray!
　　　Spring over the ground,
　　　Like a hunting-hound!
For this is Thanksgiving Day.

Over the river and through the wood,
　And straight through the barn-yard gate.
　　　We seem to go
　　　Extremely slow,—
It is so hard to wait!

Over the river and through the wood—
　Now grandmother's cap I spy!
　　　Hurrah for the fun!
　　　Is the pudding done?
Hurrah for the pumpkin-pie!

RALPH WALDO EMERSON
1803–1882

Fable

The mountain and the squirrel
Had a quarrel;
And the former called the latter "Little
    Prig."
Bun replied,
"You are doubtless very big;
But all sorts of things and weather
Must be taken in together,
To make up a year
And a sphere.

And I think it no disgrace
To occupy my place.
If I'm not so large as you,
You are not so small as I,
And not half so spry.
I'll not deny you make
A very pretty squirrel track;
Talents differ; all is well and wisely put;
If I cannot carry forests on my back,
Neither can you crack a nut."

HENRY WADSWORTH LONGFELLOW
1807–1882

The Village Blacksmith

Under a spreading chestnut-tree
  The village smithy stands;
The smith, a mighty man is he,
  With large and sinewy hands;
And the muscles of his brawny arms
  Are strong as iron bands.

His hair is crisp, and black, and long,
  His face is like the tan;
His brow is wet with honest sweat,
  He earns whate'er he can,
And looks the whole world in the face,
  For he owes not any man.

Week in, week out, from morn till night,
  You can hear his bellows blow;
You can hear him swing his heavy
  sledge,
  With measured beat and slow,
Like a sexton ringing the village bell,
  When the evening sun is low.

And children coming home from school
  Look in at the open door;
They love to see the flaming forge,
  And hear the bellows roar,
And catch the burning sparks that fly
  Like chaff from a threshing-floor.

He goes on Sunday to the church,
  And sits among his boys;
He hears the parson pray and preach,
  He hears his daughter's voice,
Singing in the village choir,
  And it makes his heart rejoice.

It sounds to him like her mother's
  voice,
  Singing in Paradise!
He needs must think of her once more,
  How in the grave she lies;
And with his hard, rough hand he wipes
  A tear out of his eyes.

Toiling,—rejoicing,—sorrowing,
    Onward through life he goes;
Each morning sees some task begin,
    Each evening sees it close;
Something attempted, something
        done,
    Has earned a night's repose.

Thanks, thanks to thee, my
        worthy friend,
    For the lesson thou hast taught!
Thus at the flaming forge of life
    Our fortunes must be wrought;
Thus on its sounding anvil shaped
    Each burning deed and thought.

JOHN GREENLEAF WHITTIER
1807–1892

Barbara Frietchie

Up from the meadows rich with corn,
Clear in the cool September morn,

The clustered spires of Frederick stand
Green-walled by the hills of Maryland.

Round about them orchards sweep,
Apple and peach tree fruited deep,

Fair as the garden of the Lord
To the eyes of the famished rebel horde,

On that pleasant morn of the early fall
When Lee marched over the mountain-
  wall;

Over the mountains winding down,
Horse and foot, into Frederick town.

Forty flags with their silver stars,
Forty flags with their crimson bars,

Flapped in the morning wind: the sun
Of noon looked down, and saw not one.

Up rose old Barbara Frietchie then,
Bowed with her fourscore years and ten;

Bravest of all in Frederick town,
She took up the flag the men hauled down,

In her attic window the staff she set,
To show that one heart was loyal yet.

Up the street came the rebel tread,
Stonewall Jackson riding ahead.

Under his slouched hat left and right
He glanced; the old flag met his sight.

"Halt!"—the dust-brown ranks stood
  fast.
"Fire!"—out blazed the rifle-blast.

It shivered the window, pane and sash;
It rent the banner with seam and gash.

Quick, as it fell, from the broken staff
Dame Barbara snatched the silken scarf.

She leaned far out on the window-sill,
And shook it forth with a royal will.

"Shoot, if you must, this old gray head,
But spare your country's flag," she said.

A shade of sadness, a blush of shame,
Over the face of the leader came;

The nobler nature within him stirred
To life at that woman's deed and word;

"Who touches a hair of yon gray head
Dies like a dog! March on!" he said.

All day long through Frederick street
Sounded the tread of marching feet:

All day long that free flag tost
Over the heads of the rebel host.

Ever its torn folds rose and fell
On the loyal winds that loved it well;

And through the hill-gaps sunset light
Shone over it with a warm good-night.

Barbara Frietchie's work is o'er,
And the Rebel rides on his raids no
    more.

Peace and order and beauty draw
Round thy symbol of light and law;

And ever the stars above look down
On thy stars below in Frederick town!

Honor to her! and let a tear
Fall, for her sake, on Stonewall's bier.

Over Barbara Frietchie's grave,
Flag of Freedom and Union, wave!

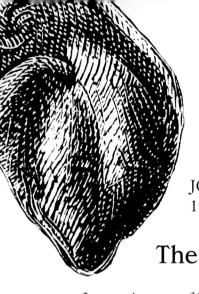

JOHN GODFREY SAXE
1816–1887

The Blind Men and the Elephant

It was six men of Indostan
  To learning much inclined,
Who went to see the Elephant
  (Though all of them were blind),
That each by observation
  Might satisfy his mind.

The *First* approached the Elephant,
  And happening to fall
Against his broad and sturdy side,
  At once began to bawl:
"God bless me! but the Elephant
  Is very like a wall!"

The *Second*, feeling of the tusk,
  Cried, "Ho! what have we here
So very round and smooth and sharp?
  To me 'tis mighty clear
This wonder of an Elephant
  Is very like a spear!"

The *Third* approached
  the animal,
  And happening to take
The squirming trunk within his hands,
  Thus boldly up and spake:
"I see," quoth he, "the Elephant
  Is very like a snake!"

The *Fourth* reached out an eager hand,
  And felt about the knee.
"What most this wondrous beast is like
  Is mighty plain," quoth he;
"'Tis clear enough the Elephant
  Is very like a tree!"

The *Fifth* who chanced to touch the ear,
  Said: "E'en the blindest man
Can tell what this resembles most;
  Deny the fact who can,
This marvel of an Elephant
  Is very like a fan!"

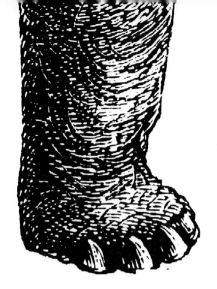

The *Sixth* no sooner had begun
    About the beast to grope,
Than, seizing on the swinging tail
    That fell within his scope,
"I see," quoth he, "the Elephant
    Is very like a rope!"

And so these men of Indostan
    Disputed loud and long,
Each in his own opinion
    Exceeding stiff and strong.
Though each was partly in the right,
    And all were in the wrong!

Moral

So oft in theologic wars,
    The disputants, I ween,
Rail on in utter ignorance
    Of what each other mean,
And prate about an Elephant
    Not one of them has seen!

EMILY DICKINSON
1830–1886

I'm nobody, who are you?
Are you nobody too?
Then there's a pair of us.
Don't tell—they'd banish us, you know.

How dreary to be somebody.
How public—like a frog—
To tell your name the livelong June
To an admiring bog.

There is no frigate like a book
    To take us to lands away,
Nor any coursers like a page
    Of prancing poetry.

This traverse may the poorest take
    Without oppress of toll;
How frugal is the chariot
    That bears a human soul!

HENRY S. LEIGH
1837–1883

The Twins

In form and feature, face and limb,
  I grew so like my brother,
That folks got taking me for him,
  And each for one another.
It puzzled all our kith and kin,
  It reached an awful pitch;
For one of us was born a twin,
  Yet not a soul knew which.

One day (to make the matter worse),
  Before our names were fixed,
As we were being washed by the nurse
  We got completely mixed;
And thus, you see, by Fate's decree,
  (Or rather, nurse's whim),
My brother John got christened *me*,
  And I got christened *him*.

This fatal likeness even dogged
  My footsteps when at school,
And I was always getting flogged,
  For John turned out a fool.
I put this question hopelessly
  To every one I knew—
What *would* you do, if you were me,
  To prove that you were *you*?

Our close resemblance turned the tide
  Of my domestic life;
For somehow my intended bride
  Became my brother's wife,
In short, year after year the same
  Absurd mistakes went on;
And when I died—the neighbors came
  And buried brother John!

PALMER COX
1840–1924

The Lazy Pussy

There lives a good-for-nothing cat,
  So lazy it appears,
That chirping birds can safely come
  And light upon her ears.

And rats and mice can venture out
  To nibble at her toes,
Or climb around and pull her tail,
  And boldly scratch her nose.

Fine servants brush her silken coat
  And give her cream for tea;—
Yet she's a good-for-nothing cat,
  As all the world may see.

The Mouse's Lullaby

Oh, rock-a-by, baby mouse, rock-a-by, so!
When baby's asleep to the baker's I'll go,
And while he's not looking I'll pop from a hole,
And bring to my baby a fresh penny roll.

CHARLES E. CARRYL
1841–1920

The Camel's Complaint

Canary-birds feed on sugar and seed,
  Parrots have crackers to crunch;
And as for the poodles, they tell me the
  noodles
  Have chicken and cream for their
  lunch.
        But there's never a question
        About *my* digestion—
            Anything does for me.

Cats, you're aware, can repose in a chair,
  Chickens can roost upon rails;
Puppies are able to sleep in a stable,
  And oysters can slumber in pails.
        But no one supposes
        A poor camel dozes—
            Any place does for me.

Lambs are enclosed where it's never
  exposed,
  Coops are constructed for hens;
Kittens are treated to houses well
  heated,
  And pigs are protected by pens.
        But a camel comes handy
        Wherever it's sandy—
            Anywhere does for me.

People would laugh if you rode a giraffe,
  Or mounted the back of an ox;
It's nobody's habit to ride on a rabbit,
  Or try to bestraddle a fox.
        But as for a camel, he's
        Ridden by families—
            Any load does for me.

A snake is as round as a hole in the
  ground,
  And weasels are wavy and sleek;
And no alligator could ever be straighter
  Than lizards that live in a creek.
        But a camel's all lumpy
        And bumpy and humpy—
            Any shape does for me.

JAMES WHITCOMB RILEY
1849–1916

Little Orphant Annie

Little Orphant Annie's come to our house to stay,
An' wash the cups an' saucers up, an' brush the crumbs away,
An' shoo the chickens off the porch, an' dust the hearth, an' sweep,
An' make the fire, an' bake the bread, an' earn her board-an'-keep;
An' all us other childern, when the supper things is done,
We set around the kitchen fire an' has the mostest fun
A-list'nin' to the witch-tales 'at Annie tells about,
An' the Gobble-uns 'at gits you
            Ef you
                    Don't
                            Watch
                                    Out!

Onc't they was a little boy wouldn't say his prayers,—
So when he went to bed at night, away up the stairs,
His Mammy heerd him holler, an' his Daddy heerd him bawl,
An' when they turn't the kivvers down, he wasn't there at all!
An' they seeked him in the rafter-room, an' cubby-hole, an' press,
An' seeked him up the chimbly-flue, an' ever'wheres, I guess;
But all they ever found was thist his pants an' roundabout—
An' the Gobble-uns'll git you
            Ef you
                    Don't
                            Watch
                                    Out!

An' one time a little girl 'ud allus laugh an' grin,
An' make fun of ever'one, an' all her blood an' kin;
An' onc't, when they was "company," an' ole folks was there,
She mocked 'em an' shocked 'em, an' said she didn't care!
An' thist as she kicked her heels, an' turn't to run an' hide,
They was two great big Black Things a-standin' by her side,
An they snatched her through the ceilin' 'fore she knowed what she's about!
An' the Gobble-uns'll git you
            Ef you
                    Don't
                            Watch
                                    Out!

An' little Orphant Annie says when the blaze is blue,
An' the lamp-wick sputters, an' the wind goes *woo—oo!*
An' you hear the crickets quit, an' the moon is gray,
An' the lightnin'-bugs in dew is all squenched away,—
You better mind yer parents, an' yer teachers fond an' dear,
An' churish them 'at loves you, an' dry the orphant's tear,
An' he'p the pore an' needy ones 'at clusters all about,
Er the Gobble-uns'll git you
            Ef you
                    Don't
                            Watch
                                    Out!

ANONYMOUS AFRICAN AMERICAN

The Origin of the Snake

Up the hill and down the level!
Up the hill and down the level!
Granny's puppy treed the Devil.

Puppy howl, and Devil shake!
Puppy howl, and Devil shake!
Devil leave, and there's your snake.

Mash his head: the sun shine bright!
Mash his head: the sun shine bright!
Tail don't die until it's night.

Night come on, and spirits groan!
Night come on, and spirits groan!
Devil come and gets his own.

EUGENE FIELD
1850–1895

Wynken, Blynken, and Nod

Wynken, Blynken, and Nod one night
  Sailed off in a wooden shoe—
Sailed on a river of crystal light,
  Into a sea of dew.
"Where are you going, and what do you wish?"
  The old moon asked the three.
  "We have come to fish for the herring fish
  That live in this beautiful sea;
  Nets of silver and gold have we!"
          Said Wynken,
          Blynken,
          And Nod.

The old moon laughed and sang a song,
  As they rocked in the wooden shoe,
And the wind that sped them all night long
  Ruffled the waves of dew.
The little stars were the herring fish
  That lived in that beautiful sea—
  "Now cast your nets wherever you wish—
  Never afeard are we";
  So cried the stars to the fishermen three:
          Wynken,
          Blynken,
          And Nod.

All night long their nets they threw
   To the stars in the twinkling foam—
Then down from the skies came the wooden shoe,
   Bringing the fishermen home;
'Twas all so pretty a sail it seemed
   As if it could not be,
And some folks thought 'twas a dream they'd dreamed
   Of sailing that beautiful sea—
   But I shall name you the fishermen three:
         Wynken,
         Blynken,
         And Nod.

Wynken and Blynken are two little eyes,
   And Nod is a little head,
And the wooden shoe that sailed the skies
   Is the wee one's trundle-bed.
So shut your eyes while mother sings
   Of wonderful sights that be,
And you shall see the beautiful things
   As you rock in the misty sea,
   Where the old shoe rocked the fishermen three:
         Wynken,
         Blynken,
         And Nod.

LAURA E. RICHARDS
1850–1943

Antonio

Antonio, Antonio,
Was tired of living alonio.
  He thought he would woo
  Miss Lissamy Loo
Miss Lissamy Lucy Molonio.

Antonio, Antonio,
Rode off on his polo-ponio.
  He found the fair maid
  In a bowery shade,
A-sitting and knitting alonio.

Antonio, Antonio,
Said, "If you will be my ownio,
  I'll love you true,
  And I'll buy for you,
An icery creamery conio!"

"Oh, nonio, Antonio! . . .
You're far too bleak and bonio!
  And all that I wish,
  You singular fish,
Is that you will quickly begonio."

Antonio, Antonio,
He uttered a dismal moanio;
  Then ran off and hid
  (Or I'm told that he did)
In the Anticatarctical Zonio.

Eletelephony

Once there was an elephant,
Who tried to use the telephant—
No! No! I mean an elephone
Who tried to use the telephone—
(Dear me! I'm not certain quite
That even now I've got it right.)

Howe'er it was, he got his trunk
Entangled in the telephunk;
The more he tried to get it free,
The louder buzzed the telephee—
(I fear I'd better drop the song
Of elephop and telephong!)

MARY E. WILKINS FREEMAN
1852–1930

The Ostrich
Is a Silly Bird

The ostrich is a silly bird,
    With scarcely any mind,
He often runs so very fast,
    He leaves himself behind.

And when he gets there, has to stand
    And hang about till night,
Without a blessed thing to do
    Until he comes in sight.

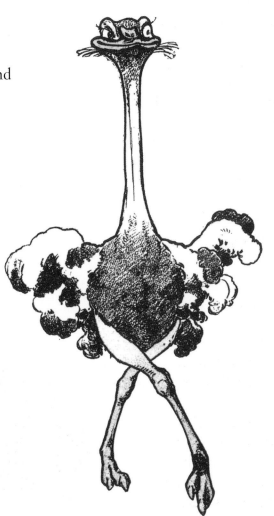

AMOS R. WELLS
1862–1933

The Considerate Crocodile

There was once a considerate crocodile
Who lay on the banks of the river Nile
And he swallowed a fish with a face of woe,
While his tears ran fast to the stream below.
"I am mourning," said he, "the untimely fate
Of the dear little fish that I just now ate!"

ERNEST LAWRENCE THAYER
1863–1940

Casey at the Bat

The outlook wasn't brilliant for the Mudville nine that day;
The score stood four to two with but one inning more to play.
And then when Cooney died at first and Barrows did the same,
A sickly silence fell upon the patrons of the game.

A straggling few got up to go in deep despair. The rest
Clung to the hope which springs eternal in the human breast;
They thought if only Casey could but get a whack at that—
We'd put up even money now with Casey at the bat.

But Flynn preceded Casey, as did also Jimmy Blake,
And the former was a lulu and the latter was a cake;
So upon that stricken multitude grim melancholy sat,
For there seemed but little chance of Casey's getting to the bat.

But Flynn let drive a single, to the wonderment of all,
And Blake, the much despisèd, tore the cover off the ball;
And when the dust had lifted, and the men saw what had occurred,
There was Jimmy safe at second and Flynn a-hugging third.

Then from five thousand throats and more there rose a lusty yell;
It rumbled through the valley, it rattled in the dell;
It knocked upon the mountain and recoiled upon the flat,
For Casey, mighty Casey, was advancing to the bat.

There was ease in Casey's manner as he stepped into his place;
There was pride in Casey's bearing and a smile on Casey's face.
And when, responding to the cheers, he lightly doffed his hat,
No stranger in the crowd could doubt 'twas Casey at the bat.

Ten thousand eyes were on him as he rubbed his hands with dirt;
Five thousand tongues applauded when he wiped them on his shirt.
Then while the writhing pitcher ground the ball into his hip,
Defiance gleamed in Casey's eye, a sneer curled Casey's lip.

And now the leather-covered sphere came hurtling through the air,
And Casey stood a-watching it in haughty grandeur there.
Close by the sturdy batsman the ball unheeded sped—
"That ain't my style," said Casey. "Strike one," the umpire said.

From the benches, black with people, there went up a muffled roar,
Like the beating of the storm waves on a stern and distant shore.
"Kill him! Kill the umpire!" shouted someone on the stand;
And it's likely they'd have killed him had not Casey raised his hand.

With a smile of Christian charity great Casey's visage shone;
He stilled the rising tumult; he bade the game go on;
He signaled to the pitcher, and once more the spheroid flew;
But Casey still ignored it, and the umpire said, "Strike two."

"Fraud!" cried the maddened thousands, and echo answered, "Fraud!"
But one scornful look from Casey and the audience was awed.
They saw his face grow stern and cold, they saw his muscles strain,
And they knew that Casey wouldn't let that ball go by again.

The sneer is gone from Casey's lip, his teeth are clenched in hate;
He pounds with cruel violence his bat upon the plate.
And now the pitcher holds the ball, and now he lets it go,
And now the air is shattered by the force of Casey's blow.

Oh, somewhere in this favored land the sun is shining bright;
The band is playing somewhere, and somewhere hearts are light.
And somewhere men are laughing, and somewhere children shout;
But there is no joy in Mudville—mighty Casey has struck out.

GELETT BURGESS
1866–1951

I Wish That My Room Had a Floor

I wish that my room had a floor;
I don't care so much for a door.
But this walking around
Without touching the ground
Is getting to be quite a bore.

The Purple Cow

I never saw a Purple Cow,
 I never hope to see one,
But I can tell you, anyhow,
 I'd rather see than be one!

ARTHUR GUITERMAN
1871–1943

Habits of the Hippopotamus

The hippopotamus is strong
  And huge of head and broad of bustle;
The limbs on which he rolls along
  Are big with hippopotomuscle.

He does not greatly care for sweets
  Like ice cream, apple pie, or custard,
But takes to flavor what he eats
  A little hippopotomustard.

The hippopotamus is true
  To all his principles, and just;
He always tries his best to do
  The things one hippopotomust.

He never rides in trucks or trams,
  In taxicabs or omnibuses,
And so keeps out of traffic jams
  And other hippopotomusses.

ROBERT FROST
1874–1963

The Last Word
of a Bluebird
As Told to a Child

As I went out a Crow
In a low voice said, "Oh,
I was looking for you.
How do you do?
I just came to tell you
To tell Lesley (will you?)
That her little Bluebird
Wanted me to bring word
That the north wind last night
That made the stars bright
And made ice on the trough
Almost made him cough
His tail feathers off.

He just had to fly!
But he sent her Good-by,
And said to be good,
And wear her red hood,
And look for skunk tracks
In the snow with an ax—
And do everything!
And perhaps in the spring
He would come back and sing."

CARL SANDBURG
1878–1967

Fog

The fog comes
on little cat feet.

It sits looking
over harbor and city
on silent haunches
and then moves on.

We Must Be Polite

(Lessons for Children on How to Behave
Under Peculiar Circumstances)

1
If we meet a gorilla
what shall we do?

Two things we may do
if we so wish to do.

Speak to the gorilla,
very, very respectfully,
"How do you do, sir?"

Or, speak to him with less
distinction of manner,
"Hey, why don't you go back
where you came from?"

2
If an elephant knocks on your door
and asks for something to eat,
there are two things to say:

Tell him there are nothing but cold
victuals in the house and he will do
better next door.

Or say: We have nothing but six bushels
of potatoes—will that be enough for
your breakfast, sir?

VACHEL LINDSAY
1879–1931

The Little Turtle

There was a little turtle.
He lived in a box.
He swam in a puddle.
He climbed on the rocks.

He snapped at a mosquito.
He snapped at a flea.
He snapped at a minnow.
And he snapped at me.

He caught the mosquito.
He caught the flea.
He caught the minnow.
But he didn't catch me.

The Moon's the North Wind's Cooky
(What the Little Girl Said)

The Moon's the North Wind's cooky,
He bites it day by day,
Until there's but a rim of scraps
That crumble all away.

The South Wind is a baker.
He kneads clouds in his den,
And bakes a crisp new moon *that . . . greedy*
North . . . Wind . . . eats . . . again!

ELIZABETH MADOX ROBERTS
1886–1941

The Rabbit

When they said the time to hide was mine,
I hid back under a thick grape vine.

And while I was still for the time to pass,
A little gray thing came out of the grass.

He hopped his way through the melon bed
And sat down close by a cabbage head.

He sat down close where I could see,
And his big still eyes looked hard at me,

His big eyes bursting out of the rim,
And I looked back very hard at him.

T. S. ELIOT
1888–1965

Macavity: The Mystery Cat

Macavity's a Mystery Cat: he's called the Hidden Paw—
For he's the master criminal who can defy the Law.
He's the bafflement of Scotland Yard, the Flying Squad's despair:
For when they reach the scene of crime—*Macavity's not there!*

Macavity, Macavity, there's no one like Macavity,
He's broken every human law, he breaks the law of gravity.
His powers of levitation would make a fakir stare,
And when you reach the scene of crime—*Macavity's not there!*
You may seek him in the basement, you may look up in the air—
But I tell you once and once again, *Macavity's not there!*

Macavity's a ginger cat, he's very tall and thin;
You would know him if you saw him, for his eyes are sunken in.
His brow is deeply lined with thought, his head is highly domed;
His coat is dusty from neglect, his whiskers are uncombed.
He sways his head from side to side, with movements like a snake;
And when you think he's half asleep, he's always wide awake.

Macavity, Macavity, there's no one like Macavity,
For he's a fiend in feline shape, a monster of depravity.
You may meet him in a by-street, you may see him in the square—
But when the crime's discovered, *then Macavity's not there!*

He's outwardly respectable (They say he cheats at cards.)
And his footprints are not found in any file of Scotland Yard's.
And when the larder's looted, or the jewel-case is rifled,
Or when the milk is missing, or another Peke's been stifled,
Or the greenhouse glass is broken, and the trellis past repair—
Ay, there's the wonder of the thing! *Macavity's not there!*

And when the Foreign Office find a Treaty's gone astray,
Or the Admiralty lose some plans and drawings by the way,
There may be a scrap of paper in the hall or on the stair—
But it's useless to investigate—*Macavity's not there!*
And when the loss has been disclosed, the Secret Service say:
"It *must* have been Macavity!"—but he's a mile away.
You'll be sure to find him resting, or a-licking of his thumbs,
Or engaged in doing complicated long division sums.

Macavity, Macavity, there's no one like
   Macavity,
There never was such a Cat of such
   deceitfulness and suavity.
He always has an alibi, and one or two
   to spare:
And whatever time the deed took place—
   MACAVITY WASN'T THERE!
And they say that all the Cats whose
   wicked deeds are widely known
(I might mention Mungojerrie, I might
   mention Griddlebone)
Are nothing more than agents for the
   Cat who all the time
Just controls their operations: the
   Napoleon of Crime!

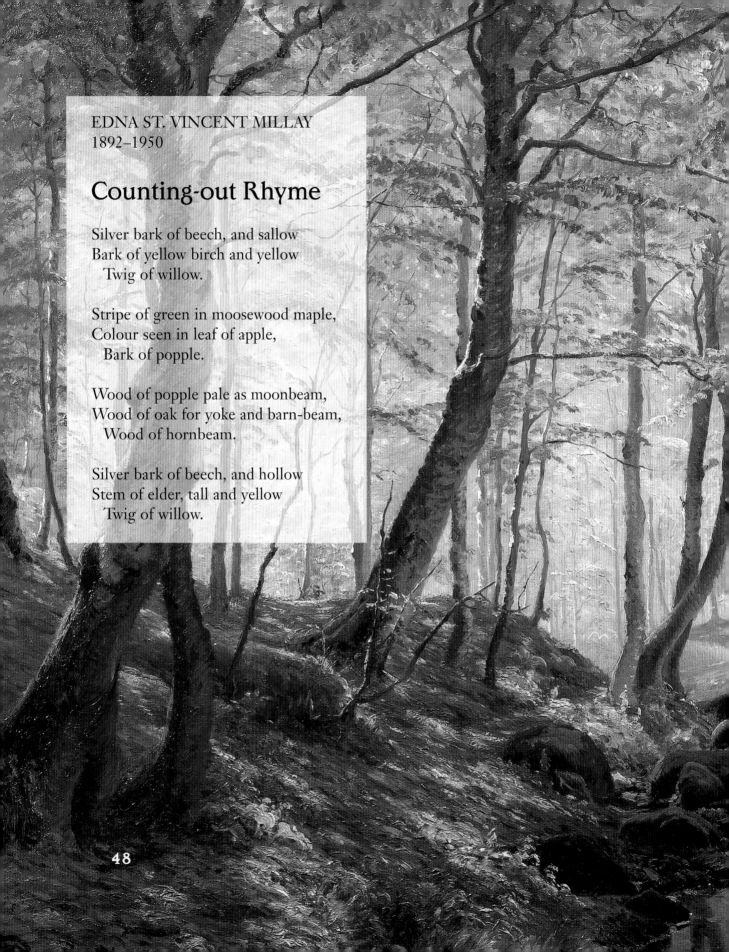

EDNA ST. VINCENT MILLAY
1892–1950

Counting-out Rhyme

Silver bark of beech, and sallow
Bark of yellow birch and yellow
  Twig of willow.

Stripe of green in moosewood maple,
Colour seen in leaf of apple,
  Bark of popple.

Wood of popple pale as moonbeam,
Wood of oak for yoke and barn-beam,
  Wood of hornbeam.

Silver bark of beech, and hollow
Stem of elder, tall and yellow
  Twig of willow.

ELIZABETH
COATSWORTH
1893–1986

No Shop Does
the Bird Use

No shop does the bird use,
no counter nor baker,
but the bush is his orchard,
the grass is his acre,
the ant is his quarry,
the seed is his bread,
and a star is his candle
to light him to bed.

49

Song of the Rabbits Outside the Tavern

We who play under the pines,
We who dance in the snow
That shines blue in the light of the
  moon
Sometimes halt as we go,
Stand with our ears erect,
Our noses testing the air,
To gaze at the golden world
Behind the windows there.

Suns they have in a cave
And stars each on a tall white stem,
And the thought of fox or night owl
Seems never to trouble them,
They laugh and eat and are warm,
Their food seems ready at hand,
While hungry out in the cold
We little rabbits stand.

But they never dance as we dance,
They have not the speed nor the grace.
We scorn both the cat and the dog
Who lie by their fireplace,
We scorn them licking their paws,
Their eyes on an upraised spoon,
We who dance hungry and wild
Under a winter's moon.

E. E. CUMMINGS
1894–1962

in Just-
spring   when the world is mud-
luscious the little
lame balloonman

whistles   far   and wee

and eddieandbill come
running from marbles and
piracies and it's
spring

when the world is puddle-wonderful

the queer
old balloonman whistles
far   and   wee
and bettyandisbel come dancing

from hop-scotch and jump-rope and

it's
spring
and
  the

          goat-footed

balloonMan   whistles
far
and
wee

RACHEL FIELD
1894–1942

Something Told the Wild Geese

Something told the wild geese
    It was time to go.
Though the fields lay golden
    Something whispered,—"Snow."
Leaves were green and stirring,
    Berries, luster-glossed,
But beneath warm feathers
    Something cautioned,—"Frost."
All the sagging orchards
    Steamed with amber spice,
But each wild breast stiffened
    At remembered ice.
Something told the wild geese
    It was time to fly,—
Summer sun was on their wings,
    Winter in their cry.

DAVID McCORD
1897–1997

Books Fall Open

Books fall open,
you fall in,
delighted where
you've never been;
hear voices not once
heard before,
reach world on world
through door on door;
find unexpected
keys to things
locked up beyond
imaginings.
What *might* you be,
perhaps *become*,
because one book
is somewhere? Some
wise delver into
wisdom, wit,
and wherewithal
has written it.
True books will venture,
dare you out,
whisper secrets,
maybe shout
across the gloom
to you in need,
who hanker for
a book to read.

OGDEN NASH
1902–1971

Adventures of Isabel

Isabel met an enormous bear,
Isabel, Isabel, didn't care.
The bear was hungry, the bear was ravenous,
The bear's mouth was cruel and cavernous.
The bear said, Isabel, glad to meet you,
How do, Isabel, now I'll eat you!
Isabel, Isabel, didn't worry,
Isabel didn't scream or scurry.
She washed her hands and straightened her hair up,
Then Isabel quietly ate the bear up.

Once in a night as black as pitch
Isabel met a wicked old witch.
The witch's face was cross and wrinkled,
The witch's gums with teeth were sprinkled.
Ho ho, Isabel! the old witch crowed,
I'll turn you into an ugly old toad!
Isabel, Isabel, didn't worry,
Isabel didn't scream or scurry.
She showed no rage and she showed no rancor,
But she turned the witch into milk and drank her.

Isabel met a hideous giant,
Isabel continued self-reliant.
The giant was hairy, the giant was horrid,
He had one eye in the middle of his forehead.
Good morning Isabel, the giant said,
I'll grind your bones to make my bread.
Isabel, Isabel, didn't worry,
Isabel didn't scream or scurry.

She nibbled the zwieback that she always fed off,
And when it was gone, she cut the giant's head off.

Isabel met a troublesome doctor,
He punched and he poked till he really shocked her.
The doctor's talk was of coughs and chills
And the doctor's satchel bulged with pills.
The doctor said unto Isabel,
Swallow this, it will make you well.
Isabel, Isabel, didn't worry,
Isabel didn't scream or scurry.
She took those pills from the pill concocter,
And Isabel calmly cured the doctor.

The Panther

The panther is like a leopard,
Except it hasn't been peppered.
Should you behold a panther crouch,
Prepare to say Ouch.
Better yet, if called by a panther,
Don't anther.

LANGSTON HUGHES
1902–1967

Mother to Son

Well, son, I'll tell you:
Life for me ain't been no crystal stair.
It's had tacks in it,
And splinters,
And boards torn up,
And places with no carpet on the floor—
Bare.
But all the time
I'se been a-climbin' on,
And reachin' landin's,
And turnin' corners,
And sometimes goin' in the dark
Where there ain't been no light.
So, boy, don't you turn back.
Don't you set down on the steps
'Cause you find it kinder hard.
Don't you fall now—
For I'se still goin', honey,
I'se still climbin',
And life for me ain't been no crystal stair.

April Rain Song

Let the rain kiss you.
Let the rain beat upon your head with silver liquid drops.
Let the rain sing you a lullaby.

The rain makes still pools on the sidewalk.
The rain makes running pools in the gutter.
The rain plays a little sleep-song on our roof at night—

And I love the rain.

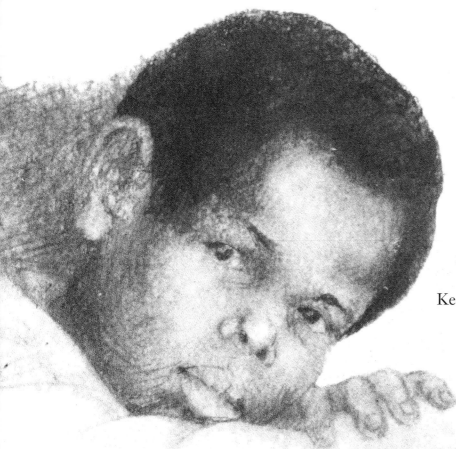

Hope

Sometimes when I'm lonely,
Don't know why,
Keep thinkin' I won't be lonely
By and by.

COUNTEE CULLEN
1903–1946

Incident

Once riding in old Baltimore,
  Heart-filled, head-filled with glee,
I saw a Baltimorean
  Keep looking straight at me.

Now I was eight and very small,
  And he was no whit bigger,
And so I smiled, but he poked out
  His tongue, and called me, "Nigger."

I saw the whole of Baltimore
  From May until December;
Of all the things that happened there
  That's all that I remember.

DR. SEUSS (THEODORE GEISEL)
1904–1991

Too Many Daves

Did I ever tell you that Mrs. McCave
Had twenty-three sons and she named them all Dave?
Well, she did. And that wasn't a smart thing to do.
You see, when she wants one and calls out, "Yoo-Hoo!
Come into the house, Dave!" she doesn't get *one*.
All twenty-three Daves of hers come on the run!
This makes things quite difficult at the McCaves'
As you can imagine, with so many Daves.
And often she wishes that, when they were born,
She had named one of them Bodkin Van Horn
And one of them Hoos-Foos. And one of them Snimm.
And one of them Hot-Shot. And one Sunny Jim.
And one of them Shadrack. And one of them Blinkey.
And one of them Stuffy. And one of them Stinkey.
Another one Putt-Putt. Another one Moon Face.
Another one Marvin O'Gravel Balloon Face.
And one of them Ziggy. And one Soggy Muff.
One Buffalo Bill. And one Biffalo Buff.
And one of them Sneepy. And one Weepy Weed.
And one Paris Garters. And one Harris Tweed.
And one of them Sir Michael Carmichael Zutt
And one of them Oliver Boliver Butt
And one of them Zanzibar Buck-Buck McFate . . .
But she didn't do it. And now it's too late.

PHYLLIS McGINLEY
1905–1978

Triolet Against Sisters

Sisters are always drying their hair.
  Locked into rooms, alone,
They pose at the mirror, shoulders bare,
Trying this way and that their hair,
Or fly importunate down the stair
  To answer a telephone.
Sisters are always drying their hair,
  Locked into rooms, alone.

THEODORE ROETHKE
1908–1963

The Sloth

In moving-slow he has no Peer.
You ask him something to his ear;
He thinks about it for a Year.

And, then, before he says a Word
There, upside down (unlike a Bird)
He will assume that you have Heard—

A most Ex-as-per-at-ing Lug.
But should you call his manner Smug,
He'll sigh and give his Branch a Hug;

Then off again to Sleep he goes,
Still swaying gently by his Toes,
And you just *know* he knows he knows.

Dinky

O what's the weather in a Beard?
It's windy there, and rather weird,
And when you think the sky is cleared
　—Why, there is Dirty Dinky.

Suppose you walk out in a Storm,
With nothing on to keep you warm,
And then step barefoot on a Worm
　—Of course, it's Dirty Dinky.

As I was crossing a hot hot Plain,
I saw a sight that caused me pain,
You asked me before,
I'll tell you again:
　—It *looked* like Dirty Dinky.

Last night you lay a-sleeping?
No! The room was thirty-five below;
The sheets and blankets turned to snow.
　—He'd got in: Dirty Dinky.

You'd better watch the things you do,
You'd better watch the things you do.
You're part of him; he's part of you
　—*You* may be Dirty Dinky.

JOHN CIARDI
1916–1986

About the Teeth of Sharks

The thing about a shark is—teeth,
One row above, one row beneath.

Now take a close look. Do you find
It has another row behind?

Still closer—here, I'll hold your hat:
Has it a third row behind that?

Now look in and . . . Look out! Oh my,
I'll *never* know now! Well, goodbye.

EVE MERRIAM
1916–1992

Catch a Little Rhyme

Once upon a time
I caught a little rhyme

I set it on the floor
but it ran right out the door

I chased it on my bicycle
but it melted to an icicle

I scooped it up in my hat
but it turned into a cat

I caught it by the tail
but it stretched into a whale

I followed it in a boat
but it changed into a goat

When I fed it tin and paper
it became a tall skyscraper

Then it grew into a kite
and flew far out of sight . . .

64

GWENDOLYN BROOKS
1917–

Michael Is Afraid of the Storm

Lightning is angry in the night.
Thunder spanks our house.
Rain is hating our old elm—
It punishes the boughs.

Now, I am next to nine years old,
And crying's not for me.
But if I touch my mother's hand,
Perhaps no one will see.

And if I keep herself in sight—
Follow her busy dress—
No one will notice my wild eye.
No one will laugh, I guess.

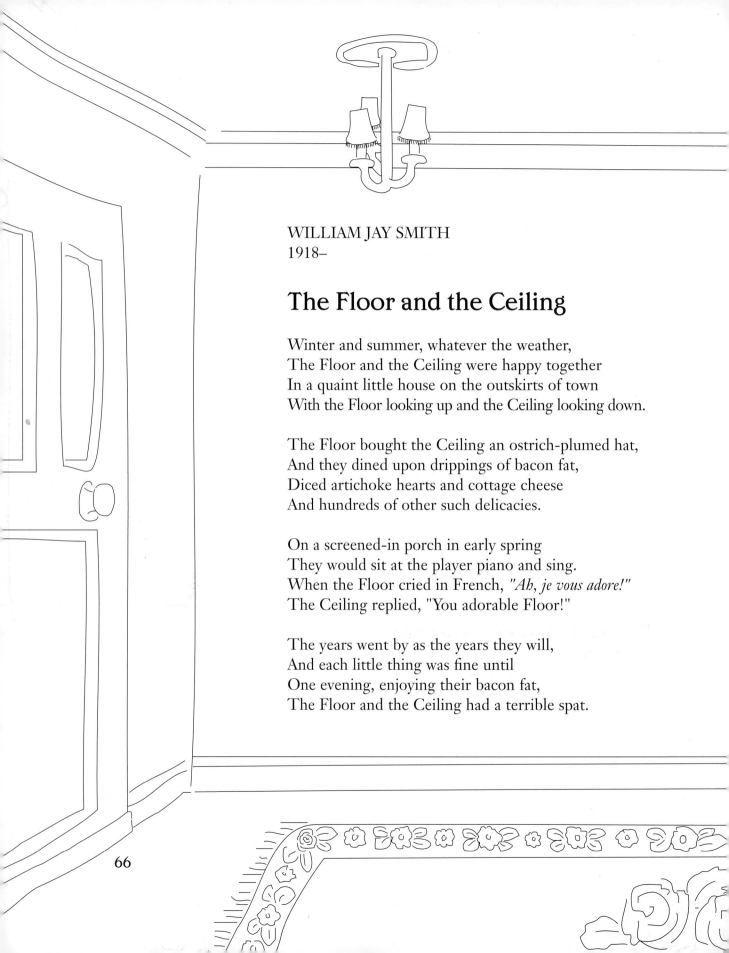

WILLIAM JAY SMITH
1918–

The Floor and the Ceiling

Winter and summer, whatever the weather,
The Floor and the Ceiling were happy together
In a quaint little house on the outskirts of town
With the Floor looking up and the Ceiling looking down.

The Floor bought the Ceiling an ostrich-plumed hat,
And they dined upon drippings of bacon fat,
Diced artichoke hearts and cottage cheese
And hundreds of other such delicacies.

On a screened-in porch in early spring
They would sit at the player piano and sing.
When the Floor cried in French, *"Ah, je vous adore!"*
The Ceiling replied, "You adorable Floor!"

The years went by as the years they will,
And each little thing was fine until
One evening, enjoying their bacon fat,
The Floor and the Ceiling had a terrible spat.

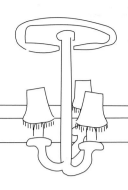

The Ceiling, loftily looking down,
Said, "You are the *lowest* Floor in this town!"
The Floor, looking up with a frightening grin,
Said, "Keep up your chatter, and *you* will cave in!"

So they went off to bed: while the Floor settled down,
The Ceiling packed up her gay wallflower gown;
And tiptoeing out past the Chippendale chair
And the gateleg table, down the stair,

Took a coat from the hook and a hat from the rack,
And flew out the door—farewell to the Floor!—
And flew out the door, and was seen no more,
And flew out the door, and *never* came back!

In a quaint little house on the outskirts of town,
Now the shutters go bang, and the walls tumble down;
And the roses in summer run wild through the room,
But blooming for no one—then why should they bloom?

For what is a Floor now that brambles have grown
Over window and woodwork and chimney of stone?
For what is a Floor when the Floor stands alone?
And what is a Ceiling when the Ceiling has flown?

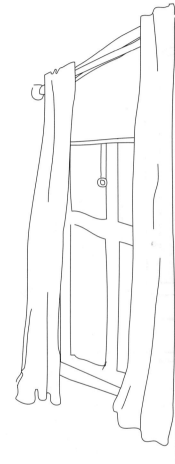

MAY SWENSON
1919–1989

Cardinal Ideograms

0
A mouth. Can blow or breathe,
be funnel, or Hello.

1
A grass blade or a cut.

2
A question seated. And a proud
bird's neck.

3
Shallow mitten for two-fingered
 hand.

4
Three-cornered hut
on one stilt. Sometimes built
so the roof gapes.

5
A policeman. Polite.
Wearing visored cap.

6
O unrolling,
tape of ambiguous length
on which is written the mystery
of everything curly.

9
Lorgnette for the right eye.
In England or if you are Alice
the stem is on the left.

7
A step,
detached from its stair.

10
A grass blade or a cut
companioned by a mouth.
Open? Open. Shut? Shut.

8
The universe in diagram:
A cosmic hourglass.
(Note enigmatic shape,
absence of any valve of origin,
how end overlaps beginning.)
Unknotted like a shoelace
and whipped back and forth,
can serve as a model of time.

RICHARD WILBUR
1921–

Some Opposites

What is the opposite of *riot?*
It's *lots of people keeping quiet.*

The opposite of *doughnut?* Wait
A minute while I meditate.
This isn't easy. Ah, I've found it!
A cookie with a hole around it.

What is the opposite of *two?*
A lonely me, a lonely you.

The opposite of a *cloud* could be
A white reflection in the sea,
Or *a huge blueness in the air*,
Caused by a cloud's not being there.

The opposite of *opposite?*
That's much too difficult. I quit.

X. J. KENNEDY
1929–

One Winter Night in August

One winter night in August
While the larks sang in their eggs,
A barefoot boy with shoes on
Stood kneeling on his legs.

At ninety miles an hour
He slowly strolled to town
And parked atop a tower
That had just fallen down.

He asked a kind old policeman
Who bit small boys in half,
"Officer, have you seen my pet
Invisible giraffe?"

"Why, sure, I haven't seen him."
The cop smiled with a sneer.
"He was just here tomorrow
And he rushed right back next year.

"Now, boy, come be arrested
For stealing frozen steam!"
And whipping out his pistol,
He carved some hot ice cream.

Just then a pack of dogfish
Who roam the desert snows
Arrived by unicycle
And shook the policeman's toes.

They cried, "Congratulations,
Old dear! Surprise, surprise!
You raced the worst, so you came in first
And you didn't win any prize!"

Then turning to the boyfoot bear,
They yelled, "He's overheard
What we didn't say to the officer!
(We never said one word!)

"Too bad, boy, we must turn you
Into a loathsome toad!
Now shut your ears and listen,
We're going to explode!"

But then, with an awful holler
That didn't make a peep,
Our ancient boy (age seven)
Woke up and went to sleep.

MARY ANN HOBERMAN
1930–

The Folk Who Live
in Backward Town

The folk who live in Backward Town
Are inside out and upside down.
They wear their hats inside their heads
And go to sleep beneath their beds.
They only eat the apple peeling
And take their walks across the ceiling.

KARLA KUSKIN
1932–

The Witches' Ride

Over the hills
Where the edge of the light
Deepens and darkens
To ebony night,
Narrow hats high
Above yellow bead eyes,
The tatter-haired witches
Ride through the skies.
Over the seas
Where the flat fishes sleep
Wrapped in the slap of the slippery deep,
Over the peaks
Where the black trees are bare,
Where boney birds quiver
They glide through the air.
Silently humming
A horrible tune,
They sweep through the stillness
To sit on the moon.

SHEL SILVERSTEIN
1932–1999

Sarah Cynthia Sylvia Stout Would Not Take the Garbage Out

Sarah Cynthia Sylvia Stout
Would not take the garbage out!
She'd scour the pots and scrape the
    pans,
Candy the yams and spice the hams,
And though her daddy would scream
    and shout,
She simply would not take the
    garbage out.
And so it piled up to the ceilings:
Coffee grounds, potato peelings,
Brown bananas, rotten peas,
Chunks of sour cottage cheese.
It filled the can, it covered the floor,
It cracked the window and blocked
    the door

With bacon rinds and chicken bones,
Drippy ends of ice cream cones,
Prune pits, peach pits, orange peel,
Gloppy glumps of cold oatmeal,
Pizza crusts and withered greens,
Soggy beans and tangerines,
Crusts of black burned buttered toast,
Gristly bits of beefy roasts . . .
The garbage rolled on down the hall,
It raised the roof, it broke the wall . . .
Greasy napkins, cookie crumbs,
Globs of gooey bubble gum,
Cellophane from green baloney,
Rubbery blubbery macaroni,
Peanut butter, caked and dry,
Curdled milk and crusts of pie,

Moldy melons, dried-up mustard,
Eggshells mixed with lemon custard,
Cold french fries and rancid meat,
Yellow lumps of Cream of Wheat.
At last the garbage reached so high
That finally it touched the sky.
And all the neighbors moved away,
And none of her friends would come to
    play.
And finally Sarah Cynthia Stout said,
"OK, I'll take the garbage out!"

But then, of course, it was too late . . .
The garbage reached across the state,
From New York to the Golden Gate.
And there, in the garbage she did hate,
Poor Sarah met an awful fate,
That I cannot right now relate
Because the hour is much too late.
But children, remember Sarah Stout,
And always take the garbage out!

NANCY WILLARD
1936–

The King of Cats Sends a Postcard to His Wife

Keep your whiskers crisp and clean.
Do not let the mice grow lean.
Do not let yourself grow fat
like a common kitchen cat.

Have you set the kittens free?
Do they sometimes ask for me?
Is our catnip growing tall?
Did you patch the garden wall?

Clouds are gentle walls that hide
gardens on the other side.
Tell the tabby cats I take
all my meals with William Blake,

lunch at noon and tea at four,
served in splendor on the shore
at the tinkling of a bell.
Tell them I am sleeping well.

Tell them I have come so far,
brought by Blake's celestial car,
buffeted by wind and rain,
I may not get home again.

Take this message to my friends.
Say the King of Catnip sends
to the cat who winds his clocks
a thousand sunsets in a box,

to the cat who brings the ice
the shadows of a dozen mice
(serve them with assorted dips
and eat them like potato chips),

and to the cat who guards his door
a net for catching stars, and more
(if with patience he abide):
catnip from the other side.

M ZELDIS 81.

SONIA SANCHEZ
1934–

To P. J. (2 yrs old who sed write a poem for me in Portland, Oregon)

if i cud ever write a
poem as beautiful as u
little 2/yr/old/brotha,
i wud laugh, jump, leap
up and touch the stars
cuz u be the poem i try for
each time i pick up a pen and paper.
u. and Morani and Mungu
be our blue/blk/stars that
will shine on our lives and
makes us finally B E.
if i cud ever write a poem as beautiful
as u, little 2/yr/old/brotha,
poetry wud go out of bizness.

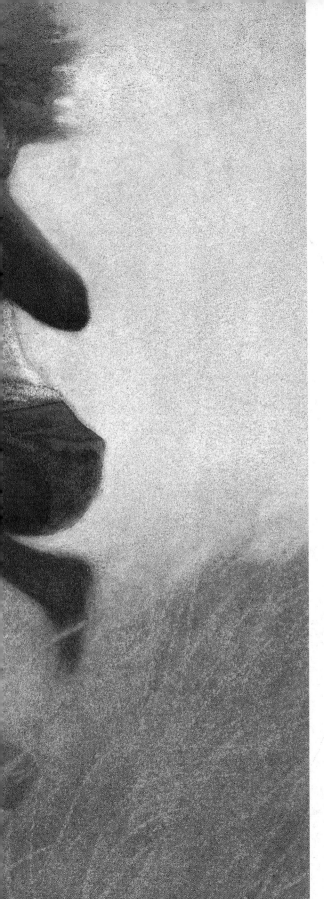

LUCILLE CLIFTON
1936–

listen children

listen children
keep this in the place
you have for keeping
always
keep it all ways

we have never hated black

listen
we have been ashamed
hopeless   tired   mad
but always
all ways
we loved us

we have always loved each other
children   all ways

pass it on

JACK PRELUTSKY
1940–

The Pancake Collector

Come visit my pancake collection,
it's unique in the civilized world.
I have pancakes of every description,
pancakes flaky and fluffy and curled.

I have pancakes of various sizes,
pancakes regular, heavy and light,
underdone pancakes and overdone
   pancakes,
and pancakes done perfectly right.

I have pancakes locked up in the closets,
I have pancakes on hangers and hooks.
They're in bags and in boxes and
   bureaus,
and pressed in the pages of books.

There are pretty ones sewn to the
   cushions
and tastefully pinned to the drapes.
The ceilings are coated with pancakes,
and the carpets are covered with crepes.

I have pancakes in most of my pockets,
and concealed in the linings of suits.
There are tiny ones stuffed in my
   mittens
and larger ones packed in my boots.

I have extras of most of my pancakes,
I maintain them in rows on these
   shelves,
and if you say nice things about them,
you may take a few home for yourselves.

I see that you've got to be going,
Won't you let yourselves out by the
   door?
It is time that I pour out the batter
and bake up a few hundred more.

PAT MORA
1942–

Castanet Clicks

Uno, dos
one, two
baskets blue.

Tres, cuatro
three, four
one bell more.

Cinco, seis
five, six
castanet clicks.

Siete, ocho
seven, eight
copper plates.

Nueve, diez
nine, ten
count again.

Tall Walking Woman

The sun stares
down with two amber eyes
on the woman, grandchildren
near her knees, who walks tall
to the slow drum beat
of her heart,
a turquoise umbrella above
her head, her blouse, the red
of soft, summer plums,
her skirt, the lavender of rain
    clouds.

Without turning her head,
the woman watches a teenager
braiding her grandmother's hair
in the shade and young girls
practicing a harvest dance.
Umbrella above her head,
the woman in the plum
red blouse, grandchildren
near her knees, in rain clouds
walks tall through the pueblo,
to a slow drum beat
in her purple tennis shoes.

82

NIKKI GIOVANNI
1943–

Knoxville, Tennessee

I always like summer
best
you can eat fresh corn
from daddy's garden
and okra
and greens
and cabbage
and lots of
barbecue
and buttermilk
and homemade ice-cream
at the church picnic

and listen to
gospel music
outside
at the church
homecoming
and go to the mountains with
your grandmother
and go barefooted
and be warm
all the time
not only when you go to bed
and sleep

GARY SOTO
1952–

Ode to Señor Leal's Goat

In the back yard
With three red
Chickens, the goat
With a tin can
For a bell drinks
From a rain puddle.
The puddle reflects
A blue sky, some clouds,
And the goat's tongue
Darting in and out.
When Señor Leal
Comes down the back
Porch, the goat looks
Up and nods his head.
The bell clangs,
And the chickens
Look up, heads cocked,
Strut and follow
The goat. The goat
Gets a carrot
And the chickens get
Clapping hands
That scare them away.
Chickens go back to
Pecking at the sandy
  ground.
Señor Leal feeds
His goat, and
Then lights his pipe.
Señor Leal, breathing in,

Looks at the sky,
Blue as an egg,
And feels good.
It's early morning.
The wind from
Some faraway mountain
Has reached him.
Señor Leal inhales
On his pipe
And then admires
The sky some more.
The goat, not knowing
Better, grabs the pipe
From Señor Leal's hand.

Señor Leal yells,
"Qué pasó?" The goat,
With pipe hanging
From his mouth,
Runs around the yard,
Through the patch
Of chiles and tomatoes,
The purple of
Eggplants. "Hey,"
Señor Leal yells.
The goat can't baa,
Because his lips
Are gripping the pipe—
A funny sight for
The chickens,
Who stay clear.
When Señor Leal
Finally grabs his goat,
The pipe is smoked.
And the goat's eyes
Are spinning from
The dizzy breath
Of man's bad habit.

FRANCISCO X. ALARCON
1954–

Jitomates Risueños

en el jardín
plantamos
jitomates

los vegetales
más felices
de todos

alegres
se redondean
de sabor

Laughing Tomatoes

risueños
se ponen
colorados

convirtiendo
sus arbustos
alambrados

en árboles
de Navidad
en primavera

in our backyard
we plant
tomatoes

the happiest
of all
vegetables

with joy
they grow round
with flavor

laughing
they change
to red

turning
their wire-framed
bushes

into
Christmas trees
in spring

Sol matutino

calentando
mi cama
en la mañana

el Sol
me llama
por la ventana

"despierta
levántate
ven afuera"

86

Morning Sun

warming up
my bed
in the morning

the Sun
calls me
through the window

"wake up
get up
come on out"

SANDRA CISNEROS
1954–

Good Hot Dogs
For Kiki

Fifty cents apiece
To eat our lunch
We'd run
Straight from school
Instead of home
Two blocks
Then the store
That smelled like steam
You ordered
Because you had the money
Two hot dogs and two pops for here

Everything on the hot dogs
Except pickle lily
Dash those hot dogs
Into buns and splash on
All that good stuff
Yellow mustard and onions
And french fries piled on top all
Rolled up in a piece of wax
Paper for us to hold hot
In our hands
Quarters on the counter

Sit down
Good hot dogs
We'd eat
Fast till there was nothing left
But salt and poppy seeds even
The little burnt tips
Of french fries
We'd eat
You humming
And me swinging my legs

JANET S. WONG
1962–

Good Luck Gold

When I was a baby
one month old,
my grandparents gave me
good luck gold:
a golden ring
so soft it bends,
a golden necklace
hooked at the ends,
a golden bracelet
with coins that say
I will be rich
and happy someday.

I wish that gold
would work
real soon.
I need my luck
this afternoon.

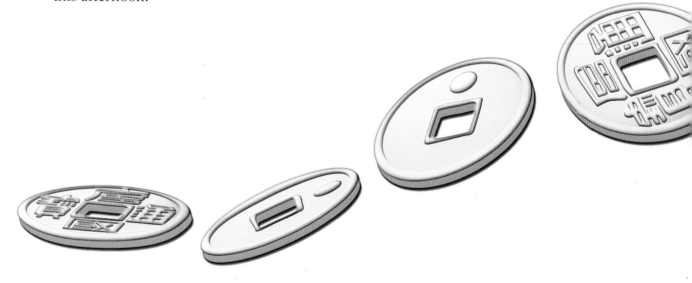

One to Ten

Yut yee sam see
Count in Cantonese with me!

Eun look chut bot
Can you tell me what we've got?

Gow sup. One to ten!
(Could you say that once again?)

Index of Authors

Index of First Lines and Titles

Ogden Nash: "Adventures of Isabel" from *The Bad Parents' Garden of Verse* by Ogden Nash. Copyright 1936 by Ogden Nash. "The Panther" from *The Bad Parents' Garden of Verse* by Ogden Nash. Copyright 1940 by Ogden Nash; first appeared in *The Saturday Evening Post*. By permission of Little, Brown and Company (Inc.).

Native American: The adaptations by Brian Swann of "Mother's Song to a Baby" from *Song of the Sky: Versions of Native American Song-Poems*, (University of Massachusetts Press, 1993) and of "She Will Gather Roses" from *Native American Songs and Poems: An Anthology* (Dover Publications, 1997) are reprinted by permission of Brian Swann.

Jack Prelutsky: "The Pankake Collector" from *The Queen of Eeen* by Jack Prelutsky. Text copyright ©1970, 1978 by Jack Prelutsky. By permission of Greenwillow Books, a division of William Morrow & Co., Inc.

Laura E. Richards: "Eletelephony" from *Tirra Lirra* by Laura E. Richards. Copyright 1930, 1932 by Laura E. Richards; copyright © 1960 by Hamilton E. Richards. By permission of Little, Brown and Company (Inc.).

Elizabeth Madox Roberts: "The Rabbit," from *Under the Tree* by Elizabeth Madox Roberts. Copyright 1922 by B. W. Huebsch, Inc., renewed 1950 by Ivor S. Roberts. Copyright 1930 by Viking Penguin, Inc., renewed © 1958 by Ivor S. Roberts. Used by permission of Viking Penguin, a division of Penguin Putnam Inc.

Theodore Roethke: "Dinky," copyright 1953 by Theodore Roethke. "The Sloth," copyright 1950 by Theodore Roethke, from *The Collected Poems of Theodore Roethke* by Theodore Roethke. Used by permission of Doubleday, a division of Random House, Inc.

Sonia Sanchez: "To P. J. (2 yrs old sed write a poem for me in Portland, Oregon)" from *It's A New Day* by Sonia Sanchez. Permission granted by Broadside Press.

Carl Sandburg: "Fog" from *Chicago Poems* by Carl Sandburg, copyright 1916 by Holt, Rinehart and Winston and renewed 1944 by Carl Sandburg. "We Must Be Polite" from *The Complete Poems of Carl Sandburg*, copyright © 1970, 1969, by Lilian Steichen Sandburg, Trustee. Reprinted by permission of Harcourt, Inc.

Dr. Seuss: "Too Many Daves" from *The Sneetches and Other Stories* by Dr. Seuss. TM and Copyright © 1961 and renewed 1989 by Dr. Seuss Enterprises, L. P. Reprinted by permission of Random House, Inc.

Shel Silverstein: "Sarah Cynthia Sylvia Stout Would Not Take the Garbage Out" from *Where the Sidewalk Ends* by Shel Silverstein. Copyright ©1974 by Evil Eye Music, Inc. Used by permission of HarperCollins Publishers.

William Jay Smith: "The Floor and the Ceiling" from *Laughing Time: Collected Nonsense* by William Jay Smith. Copyright © 1990 by William Jay Smith. Reprinted by permission of Farrar, Straus and Giroux, LLC.

Gary Soto: "Ode to Señor Leal's Goat" from *Neighborhood Odes*, copyright © 1992 by Gary Soto, reprinted by permission of Harcourt, Inc.

May Swenson: "Cardinal Ideograms" is reprinted with the permission of Simon & Schuster Books for Young Readers, an imprint of Simon & Schuster Children's Publishing Division, from *The Complete Poems to Solve* by May Swenson. Copyright © 1993 The Literary Estate of May Swenson.

Richard Wilbur: Poems 8, 12, 18, 22, and 39 from *Opposites: Poems and Drawings*, copyright © 1973 by Richard Wilbur, reprinted by permission of Harcourt, Inc.

Nancy Willard: "The King of Cats Sends a Postcard to His Wife" from *A Visit to William Blake's Inn*, copyright © 1981 by Nancy Willard, reprinted by permission of Harcourt, Inc.

Janet S. Wong: "One to Ten" and "Good Luck Gold" are reprinted with the permission of Margaret K. McElderry Books, an imprint of Simon & Schuster Children's Publishing Division, from *Good Luck Gold and Other Poems* by Janet S. Wong. Copyright © 1994 Janet S. Wong.

PICTURE CREDITS

Cover: Jessie Willcox Smith, from *A Child's Garden of Verses* by Robert Louis Stevenson (1905). Rutgers University Library Special Collections

Frontispiece: John R. Neill, unpublished illustration for *Treasure Island*, 1914. Collection of Natalie Neill Mather

Page 10: George Catlin, "Chee-ah-ka-tchee, Wife of Not-to-way." National Museum of American Art, Washington DC/Art Resource, NY

Page 11: Illustration from *The New England Primer* (1727). Library of Congress

Page 15: John Everett Millais, illustration from *Little Songs for Me to Sing* (1865)

Pages 16-17: Illustration from *A True History of a Little Woman, Who Found a Silver Penny* (1806). F. W. Olin Library, Mills College

Page 18: Grandma Moses, *Catching the Thanksgiving Turkey*. Copyright © 1946 (renewed 1974), Grandma Moses Properties Co., New York. Anna Mary